ZOMBO'S

SCARY

JOKES
& RIDDLES

As told to
John Skerchock

Dedicated to Max and Pete who are just learning about monsters and to Bob May who could rattle ten of these off in a minute without batting an eyelash.

This is a Horror Host series book.
Other books in this series include the following titles:
ZACHERLEY FOR PRESIDENT AGAIN
ZACHERLEY'S MIDNIGHT MONSTER TALES
ZACHERLEY'S CREATURE FEATURES

Published by:
 Dark Dungeon Enterprises
P.O. Box 733
Bellefonte, PA 16823

Skerchock, John
Zombo's Monster Jokes and Riddles
ISBN: 13-978-1-4895-8905-7

Published and printed in the United States of America

This is a FIRST edition.

Books by John Skerchock:
The Zacherley Scrapbook
The Frightful Dr. Shock
Vampira unauthorized
Interviews of the Fantastic
Zacherley Illustrated
World War I Cartoon Art of Pvt. Abian Wallgren USMC
 The Horror Host series:
Zacherley for President (Again)
Zacherley's Midnight Monster Tales
Zacherley's Creature Features
 CONDUCT UNBECOMING A Pennsylvania State Police Mystery

ACKNOWLEDGEMENTS: This book would not have been possible
without the help of the following people. The first and foremost is
Zombo. Coming out of retirement was a lot of work for this ghoul. I
am glad he had a sense of humor about it. Artist Steve Blickenstaff
who did the awesome portrait of Zombo on the next page. And new
artist Brain Seltzer for all the other incidental artwork in the tome.
Finally to Boris Karloff, Bela Lugosi, Lon Chaney Jr. & Sr., Huntz
Hall and the other stars and monsters who help make up these pictures. Thank you all.

Stephen
Blickenstaff
2012

Introduction

By

Zombo

I am Zombo and you're not! It is great to be me because I get to welcome you to my very first book of monster jokes and riddles. All of these funny little bits are real. I have performed them in the famous Bat Belt of night clubs across the Carpathian Mountains in old Transylvania. Now I bring them to you to enjoy.

With me in this special volume are too long time friends who, like me, are hosts of horror movies on television and in the theater. They are the famous Zacherley of Philadelphia and New York, and the famous Dr. Shock of Philadelphia. They shall be helping me tell the jokes to you.

Of course all of the monsters will be here: Dracula, the Mummy, the Wolfman, the Creature from the Black Lagoon, King Kong, Frankenstein, the Bride of Frankenstein, the Invisible Man, and the Phantom of the Opera.

It occurs to me that you can get your old Aurora monster models and set them down in front of you then pretend that the models are telling the jokes. Oh, I slay me!!!

Before we get to the funny business let me tell you that you will find hundreds of jokes and riddles within these pages, some scary monster drawings, and some pictures of my old friends. Plus, I have added some surprises along the way so that you will know what it feels like to be alone in the house of Zombo!!!

KONGTENTS

What's in your wallet?

ZOMBIE JOKES

Igor: Master, why don't zombies eat clowns?
Zombo: Because they taste funny, that's why.

Igor: How do you make a zombie float?
Zombo: One gallon of milk and four rotting zombies. Add a cherry on top.

Two zombies are ambling down the street. The first zombie says to the second zombie, "I'm hungry. Are you hungry?"
The second zombie answers, "I could use a bite." So the first zombie bit him.

Igor: What do you call a zombie floating in the lake?
Zombo: Bob.

Igor: What do you call a zombie with no arms or legs?
Zombo: Matt.

Zombo: Do zombies eat popcorn with their fingers?
Dr. Shock: No. They eat the fingers separately.

Zombo: Hey, all you zombies, do you want to play tennis?
Zombies: We can't.
Zombo: Why not?
Zombies: Because we don't have Annette.

Zombo: I heard that the Invisible Man had his heart broken.
Dr. Shock: Yes. He wanted to date a zombie but she wouldn't see him.

Zombo: What's the most common expression on a zombie's face?
Zacherley: Why deadpan of course.

Igor: Where do zombies go to work out?
Zombo: Why the muscle-leum of course!

Zombo: Where do zombies play billiards?
Zacherley: At their nearest ghoul hall.

Zombo: What do you call a zombie frozen in the ice.
Zacherley: I know that one. You would call him a cool ghoul.

Zombo: What kind of steps should you take if you see a zombie lurking in your house?
Dr. Shock: Big ones!

Zombo: Can a zombie catch you if you are carrying a big stick?
Dr. Shock: It depends on how fast you run when you carry it.

Zombo: Doctor, my zombie's nose fell off.
Dr. Shock: My goodness! How does he smell?
Zombo: Terrible.

    Two zombies are ambling down the street. The first zombie says to the second zombie, "I smell something funny."
    The second zombie replied, "No. You smell something terrible!"

Zombo: Last night I shot a zombie in my pajamas.
Igor: What was he doing in your pajamas?

First Zombie: Am I late for dinner?
Second Zombie: Yes, everyone's eaten.

    And then there was the zombie army that marched all day but only moved two feet. Get it?

Zombo: What happened to the zombie that went to clown school?
Igor: He was making a ghoul of himself so they let him go.

Prom king Transylvania High School class of 1938.

IGOR JOKES

Dr. Shock: Zombo, I don't think Igor has it all together.
Zombo: What are you talking about?
Dr. Shock: This morning I asked him if he could help me out.
Zombo: What did he do?
Dr. Shock: He showed me the exit.

Zombo: Igor, you should buy this new monster policy and save more on insurance.
Igor: Why do I need Moron Insurance?

Zombo: Igor, did you have a hard time learning in school?
Igor: Yes, master, I did.
Zombo: What were your three hardest years?
Igor: Eighth grade.

Zombo: Igor, where were you?
Igor: I was out getting a can of soda for Dr. Frankenstein.
Zombo: That sounds like a good trade. What do you think you can get for his monster?

Fritz: Igor, don't you hate going to work so early in the morning and coming home so late at night?
Igor: No. It's the part in the middle I can't stand.

Dr. Shock: Igor, can you tell me why there is so much water in watermelons?
Igor: Because we plant them in the spring.

Igor: I am sure glad I wasn't born in Transylvania.
Dracula: Why is that?
Igor: I don't know how to speak the language there.

Old Igor Proverb states that he who smiles when things go wrong has thought of someone to blame it on!

Dr. Shock: Igor, the Frankenstein monster has a fractured skull. What happened?
Igor: Well we were repairing the tower wall. The monster said to me, "I will hold spike, and when I nod my head, hit it with the sledgehammer." He did then I did.

Dr. Frankenstein: For this job, I am looking for someone who is responsible.
Igor: I am the right choice.
Dr. Frankenstein: Why?
Igor: At my last job, whenever something went wrong, they said I was responsible.

Dr. Shock: Zombo, I think Igor is really dumb.
Zombo: What do you mean?
Dr. Shock: He told me he was up all night studying for his blood test.
Zombo: I am not surprised. On his hearse he has a bumper sticker that reads, "Honk is you like peace and quiet."
Zacherley: This afternoon he asked me for a recipe to make ice cubes.
Roland: He wanted to keep bees but he heard he had to get hives.

Zombo: Igor, why are you staring at the mirror with your eyes shut?
Igor: I want to see what I look like when I am asleep.

Igor: Does anyone know how many cans of soda are in a six pack?

Dr. Shock: If Igor and King Kong jumped off of the Empire State Building at the same time, who would hit the bottom first?
Zombo: I don't know.
Dr. Shock: King Kong. Igor would have to stop and ask directions.

Zombo: Igor, do you know how to spell Mississippi?
Igor: Which one? The river or the state?

Zombo: I need a new laboratory assistant.
Dr. Shock: What happened to Igor?
Zombo: Yesterday I sent him to the kitchen to make diner. When the recipe said to separate two eggs he came back and asked me how far apart they should be.

Zombo: I don't mean to say that Igor is ugly but the other day he met Big Foot in the woods and Big Foot fainted.
Zacherley: The other day an organ grinder offered him a job as a monkey.
Dr. Shock: I saw him get a ticket from the police for being criminally ugly.
Fritz: Today he got kicked out of the zoo for scaring the animals.
Zombo: I heard when he was a kid playing cowboys and Indians the other kids made him the Lone Ranger so he would have to wear a mask.
Dr. Frankenstein: When he works with me I have to turn out the lights because he looks better in the dark.
Dr. Shock: Well, he does have a face that can drive women crazy, and most men too.

Igor: Master! I just saw a dog eat a frankfurter.
Zombo: What do you expect? It's a dog eat dog world out there.

MONSTER JOKES

Old Proverb states that you should scare unto others as you would have them scare you!

Zombo: I know a man who refused to pay his Exorcist.
Igor: What happened?
Zombo: He was repossessed. So be careful.

Zombo: Do you know what is more invisible than the Invisible Man?
Zacherley: His shadow.

Zombo: If you through a monster into the Atlantic Ocean, what happens?
Igor: He gets wet!

Zombo: Why can't scarecrows have any fun?
Igor: Why?
Zombo: Because they are nothing but a bunch of stuffed shirts.

I gargoyle every day!

Zombo: Where is the best place to get monsters?
Igor: At a monster sale?

Zombo: I know a monster that is so dumb that the only thing that can stay in it head for more than a day is a cold.
Zacherley: Oh yeah, well I know one that is so big he casts two shadows.

Zombo: If you put twenty monsters in your bedroom, what do you have?
Igor: A very big bedroom.

Old Proverb states that if you cannot say something good about a monster then . . . say something bad! It keeps the conversation going.

Igor: Do monsters kiss?
Zombo: Yes, but never on the first date.

Zombo: Have you seen Quasimodo lately?
Dr. Shock: Yes. He returned from his trip yesterday.
Zombo: Good. I had a hunch he's back.

Zombo: What is a monster's favorite game?
Igor: Hide and Shriek?

You put your left foot in, you take your left foot out. You do the hokey pokey and you shake it . . .

Igor: Master! Master, I just saw a blue monster!
Zombo: Igor, you should have done something to cheer him up!

Zombo: What monster likes to disco?
Igor: The Boogieman.

Dr. Shock: How was the monster party?
Zombo: Terrible. We ran out of food.
Dr. Shock: Why?
Zombo: Everyone was goblin.

Zombo: What is a monster's favorite bean?
Igor: A human bean.

Zombo: What song won the Monsters' Academy Awards?
Igor: I have no idea.
Zombo: it was Goon River.
Igor: I thought it would be Spook To Me of Love.

Zombo: Igor, what it the difference between a hamburger and a bag of manure?
Igor: I don't know.
Zombo: Then you are never going to make my lunch again.

Zacherley: I've had many great girlfriends over the years. A lot of them are going to be sorry when I get married.
Igor: Really? How many of them do you plan to marry?

Igor: What is the difference between a monster and candy?
Zombo: Human beings eat candy.

Zombo: What do you give a monster that has everything?
Igor: Everything that's left.

Zombo: What do you do if a monster climbs through your window?
Igor: Run out the door.

Igor: What key do monsters sing in?
Zombo: The skeleton key.

Dr. Shock: Where can I buy a dead mouse?
Igor: In a Mouse-o-leum!

Zombo: Did you hear the good news?
Dr. Shock: What is it?
Zombo: The Hunchback just became a father.
Dr. Shock: Wow! That makes him a real ding dong daddy!

"The next time we dance, I think I should lead."

Igor: What's small and green but has big yellow teeth?
Zombo: I don't know. What's small and green and has big yellow teeth?
Igor: I don't know either, but there's one crawling on your shoulder.

Igor: What food do demons eat?
Zombo: Why filet of soul of course.

Zombo: I heard there was a monster at the Graveyard Picnic who won the three legged race.
Igor: Yes. And he didn't need a partner.

SIGN ON FORTUNE TELLER'S DOOR:
Closed due to unforeseen circumstances.

Zombo: Igor, we must do something about the rats in this castle!
Igor: What can we do?
Zombo: I don't know, but there aren't enough of them.

Zacherley: I see those annoying gypsy moths are back again.
Zombo: They don't bother me as long as they stay in the trees.
Zacherley: I can't stand it the way they play those little violins!

Zombo: Igor, what does our moat monster like to eat?
Igor: He likes Moat Meal.

When breath mints become important!

Dr. Shock: I hear the monsters were kind of rowdy at the Thanksgiving Day party.
Zombo: Yes. They were all fighting over the witch bone.

Zombo: I read in the paper today that there was a riot at the opera house and they don't know who caused it.
Igor: I do. It was the Phantom of the Uproar.

Dr. Shock: What goes "Ho! Ho! Ho!" thump?
Zombo: I don't know. What goes "Ho! Ho! Ho!" thump?
Dr. Shock: Santa laughing his head off.

Zombo: I saw you in the cemetery last night with a shovel. What were you doing?
Zacherley: I was digging up an extra player for a game of cards.
Zombo: But the cemetery is locked. How did you get in?
Zacherley: I used my skeleton key.

Zombo: How do monster fairy tales end?
Igor: How?
Zombo: With everyone living horribly even after.

Zombo: What kind of weather is best for a hearse?
Zacherley: A driving rain!

Zombo: Where do monsters go on vacation?
Igor: Lake Erie!

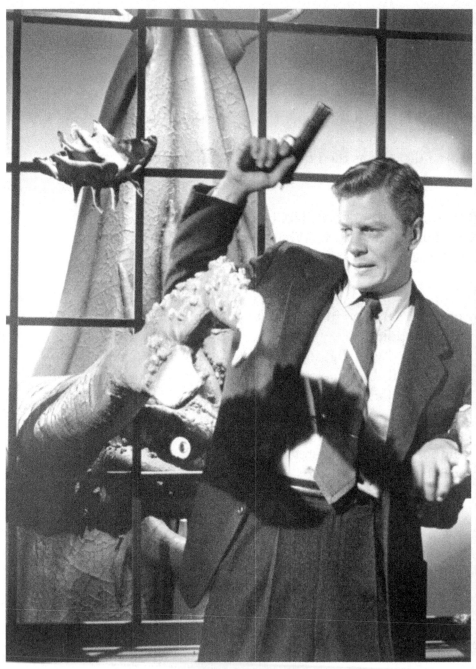

"Tag. You're it!"

Zombo: What director makes the best monster movies?
Igor: Cecil Boo DeMille.

Zombo: Who is the strongest monster in Transylvania?
Zacherley: That would be my cousin, Ghouliath.

DANGREOUS MONSTER JOBS

1. Cleaning Dracula's teeth.

2. Giving the Wolfman a haircut.

3. Giving Godzilla a pedicure.

4. Giving King Kong a shave.

5. Polishing Frankenstein's nuts.

6. Inviting a zombie over for something to eat.

This will only hurt for a minute.

MAD DOCTOR JOKES

Dr. Shock: Zombo you need to get some rest.
Zombo: I can't. My haunted house is way too noisy.
Dr. Shock: Why is that?
Zombo: It has wail to wail carpeting.

Zacherley: Doctor, what are you doing?
Dr. Shock: I'm building a giant snake.
Zacherley: Oh, you're a boa constructor.

Zombo: Did you hear about the owl with laryngitis?
Dr. Shock: No. What happened?
Zombo: He didn't give a hoot.

Zombo: What does a mad scientist grow in the garden?
Igor: Only transplants.

Zombo: How does the Hunchback get rid of a sore throat?
Igor: He gargoyles twice a day.

Igor: Doctor, what's the quickest way to cure double vision?
Dr. Shock: Shut one eye!

33

Zacherley: Doc, my friend thinks he's a cross town bus.
Dr. Shock: You'd better send him to see me.
Zacherley: I can't. He doesn't stop at your corner.

Igor: I see pink and blue spots before my eyes.
Zombo: Did you ever see an eye doctor?
Igor: No. Just pink and blue spots.

Dr. Shock: Before I give you the bad news, I must know, are you an organ donor?
Zombo: No. But I did once donate a piano to Good Will.

Zombo: Did you hear about the monster who walked into the doctor's office? He had a banana up his nose, a pineapple in one ear and a cucumber in the other.
Zacherley: What happened?
Zombo: The doctor told him that he wasn't eating properly.

Dr. Shock: Igor, I have some bad news and some worse news.
Igor: What's the bad news?
Dr. Shock: You have only 24 hours to live.
Igor: What's the worse news?
Dr. Shock: I was trying to tell you since yesterday.

Igor: Doctor, I can't keep my hands from shaking.
Dr. Shock: Do you drink a lot?
Igor: No. I spill most of it.

Hearts must be thawed properly before cooking.

Zombo: Doctor! Doctor! A scorpion just bit my leg.
Dr. Shock: Which one?
Zombo: I don't know. Scorpions all look alike to me.

Dr. Frankenstein: Igor, have you found me a brain?
Igor: No.
Dr. Frankenstein: Why not?
Igor: I was too busy looking for one for the monster.

Dr. Shock: Hey, Igor, what are you doing with that worm?
Igor: He is not a worm. He is a poet.
Dr. Shock: Well, I can see that he's a long fellow.

Zombo: Why did the mad scientist move to France?
Igor: I don't know, master
Zombo: He wanted to study the Paris sites.

Dr. Shock: Dr. Frankenstein, I hear you're moving your laboratory to the local school.
Dr. Frankenstein: No. That is too much trouble. I'll just use their assembly hall.

Zacherley: Zombo, why are you so sad?
Zombo: I was a guest speaker at the local school today.
Zacherley: And that made you sad?
Zombo: Yes.
Zacherley: What happened?
Zombo: I asked a little boy who shot Abraham Lincoln. He said he didn't know, and if he did he wouldn't squeal.
Zacherley: That is sad, but then most children won't squeal because they are taught not to get involved.

Zombo: I am sorry, Dracula, you are unable to gain any weight.
Dracula: But I've been eating extra to gain more weight.
Zombo: Well, it's all been in vein.

Dr. Shock: Did you hear about the optometrist who fell into the lens grinding machine?
Zombo: No. What happened?
Dr. Shock: He made a spectacle out of himself.

Zacherley: Doctor, what has more lives than a cat?
Dr. Shock: A frog. It croaks every night.

Zombo: Doctor, doctor, what should I take for a chest cold?
Dr. Shock: Two coffin drops twice a day.

Dr. Shock: Can you tell me what happens when a body is thoroughly immersed in water?
Vampira: In my case the telephone usually rings.

Dr. Shock: Zombo, will you let me make a clone of you.
Zombo: No.
Dr. Shock: Why not?
Zombo: Because you can't improve upon perfection.

Igor got appendicitis and had to be rushed to the hospital for an emergency operation. "Doctor! Doctor!" he cried. " I am scared. This is my first operation."

Dr. Shock looked down calmly at his patient and said, "I know how you feel. It's my first operation too."

Creature from the Black Lagoon: Doctor! Doctor! For two months now you've had me eat nothing but sardines.
Dr. Shock: Yes. How is the diet working?
Creature from the Black Lagoon: Not to well. Every time I take a dip in the lagoon I leave a ring of olive oil around it.

Going my way?

WITCH JOKES

Zombo: What's another name for a ghost ship?
Igor: A witch craft.

Zombo: Why didn't the little witch mail her letters?
Dr. Shock: She didn't want to play post office.

Zombo: Did you hear about the dumb witch?
Igor: No.
Zombo: She fired her broom for sweeping on the job.

Zombo: What do ghouls do before they blow out their birthday candles?
Zacherley: that's easy. They make a witch.

Dr. Shock: Hagatha, I see your little boy is turning into a fine monster.
Hagatha: Yes. He gruesome!

Zombo: Why did the young witch quit her job at the wool factory?
Igor: I don't know.
Zombo: Because she didn't want to dye!!!

"You look very tasty!"

Zombo: Then there was the witch that was so clumsy.
Dr. Shock: How clumsy was she?
Zombo: She was so clumsy that every time she rode her broom she'd fly off the handle.

Zombo: Did you hear about the witch that was so dumb?
Dr. Shock: No. How dumb was she?
Zombo: She was so dumb she flunked spelling!
Dr. Shock: Was this the same witch who stared at the can of orange juice for an hour?
Zombo: Why would she do that?
Dr. Shock: Because the can had "concentrate" written on it.

Old Witch: I have the face of a sixteen year old girl.
Zombo: Well you better give it back before she complains.

Witches' Motto: We came. We saw. We conjured!

Zombo: I heard that the little witch learned how to spell CAT in school yesterday.
Zacherley: Yes. And today she learned how to spell people.

Zombo: Why do witches fly on broomsticks?
Hagatha: Because vacuum cleaner cords aren't long enough.

"I'd love to have you for dinner!"

Igor: Ouch! I hurt my thumb.
Witch: Let me kiss it and make it worse.

Zombo: Did you hear about that old hag who rescued those people in the sinking boat?
Dr. Shock: Yes. I saw it in the newspaper under the headline "A Witch In Time Saves Nine!"

Hagatha: My daughter will soon be old enough to drive.
Zombo: Will you be celebrating?
Hagatha: Oh yes. We'll throw her a shriek sixteen party!

Hagatha: What do you think of poison ivy as a garden plant?
Samantha: It may not be beautiful, but it's the kind of plant that will grow on you.

Samantha: Hagatha, why aren't you married?
Hagatha: Not to worry. I can marry any man I please.
Samantha: Oh?
Hagatha: The trouble is that I can't seem to please anyone.

Hagatha: Why do you wear your wedding ring on the wrong finger?
Sadie: Because I married the wrong warlock.
Hagatha: But he seems to be a man of rare gifts.
Sadie: I'll say. He hasn't given me one since we got married five years ago.

Zombo: Am I seeing double? I can't tell either Hagatha or Sadie apart.
Sadie: You can't tell witch witch is which?

"Who forgot to lock the door?"

KING KONG JOKES

Zombo: Why was King Kong such a great actor?
Igor: Well, if you put an ape in a spotlight monkeyshines.

Zombo: Why did King Kong climb the Empire State Building?
Igor: Because the elevator was broken.

Zombo: What is King Kong's favorite food?
Igor: Banana Scream Pie!

Zombo: How does King Kong like his steaks cooked?
Chief: Medium roar.

Zombo: What did King Kong say as he tumbled from the top of the Empire State Building?
Igor: I don't know.
Zombo: He said, "Baby, I'm falling for you!"

King Kong: Knock, knock.
Zombo: Who's there?
King Kong: Boris.
Zombo: Boris who?
King Kong: Boris to death with some more jokes.

Zombo: What is the difference between King Kong and a stray dog.

Igor: I don't know.

Zombo: There are fewer fleas on the dog.

Zombo: Hey, Kong, being about thirty feet tall, what's the hardest thing you have to do everyday.

King Kong: That would be tying my shoe laces.

Igor: Max, what's wrong?

Max: I am so mad at King Kong I feel like telling him to jump in the lake again.

Igor: What do you mean by again?

Max: I felt like telling him yesterday too.

Zombo: Is it true that King Kong dropped a man fifty feet without hurting him?

Zacherley: Well, he dropped him fifty-one feet but the first fifty didn't hurt at all.

Zombo: Where does King Kong put his empty banana peels?

Igor: Where, Master?

Zombo: Anywhere he wants to. He's king kong.

Life can be a little hairy.

WOLF MAN JOKES

Zombo: What do you get if you cross the Wolf Man with an octopus?
Igor: A fur coat with a lot of sleeves.

Old Proverb states one must always remember that a fiend in need is a fiend indeed!

Zombo: What excuse did the Wolfman give for kidnapping the gorgeous girl?
Dr. Shock: He said, "I can't help it. She brings out the beast in me!"

Larry Talbot: Where do fleas go in the winter?
Wolfman: Search me.

Larry Talbot: Hey, Wolfman, how do you sign your letters?
Wolfman: I always sign them "Beast Vicious"!

Zacherley: How many werewolves does it take to change a light bulb?
Igor: What do werewolves need light bulbs for?

Igor: How many werewolves does it take to change a light bulb?
Zombo: One. But you have to howl at him to do it!

Zacherley: Hey, Wolfman, I heard you were in a play last night.
Wolfman: That's right. And it was a howling success!!

Zombo: Why do werewolves do so good in school.
Zacherley: Because they can give snappy answers.

Zacherley: What is the Wolfman's favorite meal?
Igor: Rabid Stew.

Larry: I heard that the Wolfman fell into the washing machine again.
Talbot: Yes. Now he's a wash and werewolf.

Dr. Shock: Did you ever hear the Werewolves' Curse?
Zombo: No. But if I did I'd make them wash their mouths out with soap.

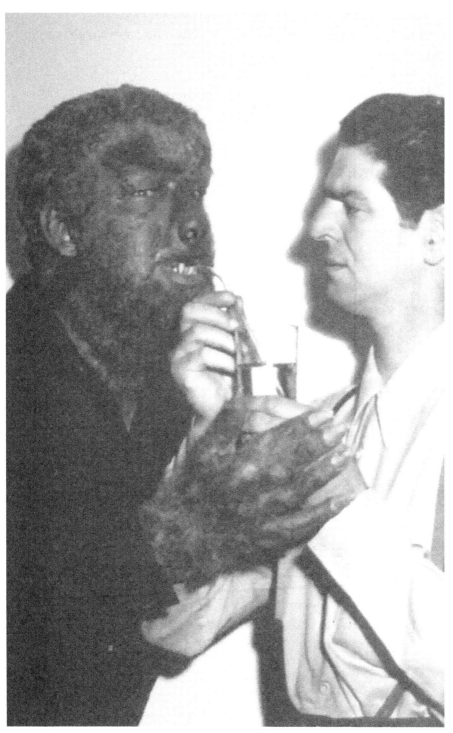

Sippy cups-not just for kids anymore.

Zombo: What did the Wolfman say when he found a Prince in his food?
Igor: What did he say?
Zombo: He said, "Waiter! There's an heir in my soup!"

Zombo: Why is Christmas like the Wolfman at the beach?
Larry Talbot: Because they both have sandy claws. Get it? Santy Claus-sandy claws? Ha. Ha.

Zombo: If you crossed a werewolf with a vampire what would you get?
Igor: I don't know.
Zombo: You'd get a fur collar that fastens to the front of your neck.
Igor: Is that rue?
Zombo: Well, you might get a mad dog that chases airplanes.

Dracula: Why is the Wolfman eating so much garlic these days?
Zombo: He wants his bark to be worse than his bite.

Dr. Shock: I think the Wolfman is having a break down.
Zombo: What do you mean?
Dr. Shock: I think the Wolfman believes he is a dog.
Zombo: What makes you say that?
Dr. Shock: last night I saw him chasing cars.

Larry: Why is the moon like a dollar?
Talbot: It's made up of four quarters.

GODZILLA JOKES

Zombo: What do you feed a hungry Godzilla?
Igor: Anything he wants!

Zombo: What is the best way to speak to Godzilla?
Igor: From as far away as possible.

Igor: What game does Godzilla like to play?
Zombo: Squash.

Zombo: How do you keep Godzilla from charging?
Igor: How?
Zombo: Take away his credit cards.

Zombo: What can you find between Godzilla's toes?
Igor: Slow runners.

Igor: What did Godzilla eat at the restaurant?
Zombo: Two waiters and the cook.

Igor: Why doesn't Godzilla invade Hong Kong?
Zombo: He doesn't like Chinese food.

Zombo: What does Godzilla call the Creature from the Black lagoon?
Igor: Sushi.

Zombo: Why did Godzilla eat all the army tanks?
Zacherley: Because I told him he needed iron in his diet!

Igor: Why did Godzilla eat the paint factory?
Zombo: He needed a little color.

Zombo: Why did Godzilla eat the lamp factory?
Igor: He was on a light diet.

Zombo: Why did Godzilla paint his toe nails red?
Igor: I don't know, master.
Zombo: He wanted to hide in a strawberry patch.

Dr. Shock: Where was Godzilla when the lights went out?
Zacherley: In the dark.

Zombo: What movie title do you think of when you look at Godzilla's underwear?
Dr. Shock: The Human Stain.

Zombo: Why couldn't Godzilla catch his own tail?
Zacherley: Because it's hard to make ends meet these days.

Zombo: Why did Godzilla eat all that dynamite for dinner?
Igor: He was hoping to get a bang out of dessert.

Igor: Master! Master! Godzilla just swallowed his knife and fork. He wants to know what he should do.
Zombo: Tell him to eat with his hands.

Igor: Master, where does Godzilla hide his Easter eggs?
Zombo: Anywhere he wants to!

Zombo says, "Boo!"

DRACULA AND VAMPIRE JOKES

Zombo: Why should you never lend money to Dracula?
Barnabas: It's dangerous to let a vampire put the bite on you.

Dr. Shock: Hey, Dracula, what's your favorite holiday?
Dracula: Why Fangsgiving of course.

Zombo: Why are vampires always so serious?
Igor: I don't know.
Zombo: because they always behave in a grave manner.
Igor: My dead uncle lives in a grave manor.
Zombo: Shut up.

Zombo: Dracula, why is your family so close?
Dracula: I am surprised you would ask. Everybody knows that blood is thicker than water.

Zombo: What's the best way to talk to Dracula?
Igor: By long distance.

"I can make myself look like the guy in the picture."

Zombo: What kind of Indians does Dracula like?
Igor: I don't know.
Zombo: Full blooded ones.

Igor: How do you make vampire stew?
Zombo: Keep him waiting until daylight.

Dr. Shock: I had to fire Count Dracula as my agent.
Zombo: Why would you ever do that?
Dr. Shock: He wanted to take more than the usual ten percent bite.

Dr. Shock: I heard Dracula lost his job at the blood bank.
Zombo: Yes. He was caught drinking on the job.

Igor: Master, I think that girl vampire likes me.
Zombo: How do you know?
Igor: Look at the way she bats her eyes.

Dracula: I used to be a policeman. I worked nights but I had to quit.
Zombo: Why is that?
Dracula: I hated stake outs. Well, I hate stakes in too, because they cause such heart burn.
Zombo: Okay, Drac, the joke's over.

"Look into my eyes and I shall give you a surprise!"

Zombo: Dracula, what do you consider fast food?
Dracula: A person with high blood pressure.

Dracula: Knock. Knock.
Victim: Who's there?
Dracula: Isle.
Victim: Isle who?
Dracula: I'll bite you on the neck as soon as you open the door and let me in.

Zacherley: You know, I heard that Dracula won't eat garlic.
Zombo: He's afraid it will give him bat breath.

Zombo: What kind of coffee does Dracula drink?
Dr. Shock: Why decoffinated of course.

Zombo: Dracula, who is the most famous nurse in Transylvania?
Dracula: It's Florence Nightinghoul.

Dr. Shock: Hey, Dracula, I hear vampires whistle in Transylvania.
Dracula: You must have good hearing. By the way, do you want to join my fang club?

Zombo: Dracula is a nice guy.
Igor: How so?
Zombo: He never says a cross word to anyone.

"What do you mean I look like Harry Potter?"

Igor: Dracula seems in a foul mood.
Zombo: He's like the rest of us. He has his good days and his bat days.

Zombo: What kinds of ships will vampires sail in?
Igor: Blood vessels.

Zombo: Did you hear about the vampire who was so dumb?
Dr. Shock: How dumb was he?
Zombo: He bought glasses for his eye teeth.

Zombo: What game do vampires like to play?
Igor: Batminton.

Zombo: What food do vampires eat when it's cold outside?
Igor: Alpha-bat soup.

Zombo: Hey, Dracula, do you want to play a game of baseball?
Dracula: No. Vampires don't like any game where you have to hit the bat.

Zombo: I heard that there was a vampire who was so dumb.
Igor: How dumb was he?
Zombo: He was so dumb that when he was told to stand in the batter's box he thought the umpire meant his coffin.
Igor: I think that was strike three, master.

"Now I will hide, and you can count to ten!"

Dracula: Doctor! Doctor! I have such terrible heartburn.
Dr. Shock: You better lay off the stakes!

Zombo: What do you have when you find vampires living in a church steeple?
Zacherley: You have bats in the belfry.
Zombo: And if you found them in the clock tower?
Zacherley: They'd be ding bats.

Dr. Shock: So, Dracula, I hear you are going to start your own airline.
Dracula: Yes. It will fly to Transylvania and back.
Dr. Shock: It sounds like a fly by night operation.

Zombo: What do you call a vampire moth?
Dracula: A myth.

Zombo: Dracula, can you turn into a bat.
Dracula: Yes. Can you turn into anything?
Zombo: I turned into a door once.
Dracula: What happened?
Zombo: I broke my nose.

Zombo: I am taking the monsters on a road trip.
Zacherley: You better let Dracula ride in the front seat.
Zombo: Why?
Zacherley: He's a terrible bat seat driver.

"Who touched my Frosted Flakes?"

Dr. Shock: Dracula, what's the matter? You don't look well.
Dracula: I had terrible nightmares. I dreamt that I was turned into a hot dog and everyone wanted a bite of me.
Dr. Shock: So you went from bat to wurst.

Zombo: Dracula, welcome. Come in and sit down. Igor, get him someone to eat.
Dracula: No thank you. I just ate necks-door.

Zombo: Did you hear? Finally a TV network is making a television series about Dracula!
Igor: Finally, a show that will suck on purpose!

FRANKENSTEIN JOKES

Zombo: What would you get if you crossed Frankenstein with a werewolf?
Igor: What?
Zombo: An electric fur coat.

Dr. Shock: Why did Frankenstein wear green suspenders?
Zombo: To keep his pants up?

Dr. Shock: Why did Frankenstein wear red suspenders?
Zombo: Because the green ones were in the wash?

Dr. Shock: Why did Frankenstein wear blue suspenders?
Zombo: Because the red ones broke?

Zombo: What does Frankenstein do to relax?
Igor: He gets his battery re-charged.
Zombo: How revolting.

Zombo: What's Frankenstein's eye color?
Igor: Shocking blue.

Migraine headache number 100!

Dr. Frankenstein: The monster had a terrible time shopping at the clothing store today.

Zombo: What happened?

Dr. Frankenstein: He asked for a fur coat for his Bride.

Zombo: That sounds nice.

Dr. Frankenstein: Yes, but the clerk misunderstood and said that they don't take trades.

Dr. Frankenstein: Did you know my monster is an excellent gardener?

Zombo: No. How is that possible?

Dr. Frankenstein: He has a green thumb.

Frankenstein: I used to be a teacher but I had to quit.

Dr. Shock: Why is that?

Frankenstein: My eyes kept falling out of their sockets.

Dr. Shock: Oh, you couldn't control your pupils.

Zacherley: So, Frankenstein, I haven't seen you or a while. Where have you been?

Frankenstein: I've been to medical school.

Zacherley: Oh, what are you studying?

Frankenstein: Nothing. They're studying me.

Zombo: What does Frankenstein like to drink on a hot summer day?

Zacherley: A nice cool glass of Ghoul-ade!

"Who keeps ringing the doorbell and running away?"

Igor: Knock. Knock.
Dr. Frankenstein: Who's there?
Igor: Robin.
Dr. Frankenstein: Robin who?
Igor: Robin graves is dangerous even at night.

Zombo: Why does Frankenstein's monster love my jokes?
Igor: Why?
Zombo: Because they keep him in stitches!

Dr. Frankenstein: My monster has become very sick.
Zombo: Did he catch a bug?
Dr. Frankenstein: Yes, a lightning bug.

Zombo: Dr. Frankenstein, did your monster ever go to college?
Dr. Frankenstein: No.
Zombo: How come?
Dr. Frankenstein: He doesn't know the way.

Monster: How do I get to college?
Zombo: Study real hard!

Dr. Frankenstein: My monster heard that Igor's friend, Fred Ricity was running for office.
Zombo: What did he do?
Dr. Frankenstein: He went to the polls and used his volt to elect Ricity.
Zombo: I'm feeling sick now.

"Where is the television remote?"

Zombo: Did the monster ever get married?

Igor: He asked for a woman's hand in marriage.

Zombo: What happened?

Igor: That's what he got, the hand.

Zombo: That's it?

Igor: The rest of her came with it but had some assembly required.

Zombo: I heard the marriage fell apart.

Igor: The glue wasn't strong enough. It broke the monster's heart.

Zombo: Oh well, he'll just have to get another one.

Igor: Master, Frankenstein just rolled his eyes at me.

Zombo: Well, play nice and roll them back.

GHOST JOKES

Igor: Why can't ghosts get dates?
Zombo: Because girls see right through them.

Old proverb states that when a ghost haunts a theater the actors will get stage fright.

Zombo: Tonight's dinner special will be a sand witch, ghoul aid, and lady fingers with whipped scream. For sea monsters we have a fish and ships special.

Zombo: Did you sell your haunted house?
Dr. Shock: No.
Zombo: How come?
Dr. Shock: My home moaner policy had expired.

Dr. Shock: Ghosts are too scared to live in my haunted house because they have no guts.
Dr. Shock: It's a shame too. Monsters would love it.
Zombo: Why is that?
Dr. Shock: It's on a dead end street.

Igor: Why don't ghosts like to take tests in school?
Zombo: Tell me.
Igor: They make too many boo boos.

Zombo: What do ghosts love Halloween?
Dr. Shock: That's when haunting season starts.
Casper: A haunting we will go. A haunting we will go. Hi-ho a spooky show, a haunting we will go.

Zombo: Why are wet ghosts so sad?
Casper: because they've had their spirits dampened.

Igor: My friend is a Scottish ghost.
Zombo: What's his name?
Igor: MacDughoul.

Casper: Why are writers the scariest creatures in the world?
Spooky: I don't know.
Casper: because their tales come out o their heads.

Ghost: Knock-knock.
Zombo: Who's there?
Ghost: Noah.
Zombo: Noah who?
Ghost: Noah Body!!

Casper: What doesn't exist but has a name?
Zombo: I don't know.
Casper: Nothing!

Zombo: What does a ghost like to drink?
Igor: I don't know.
Zombo: Evaporated milk!

Zombo: Hey, Casper, what are you reading?
Casper: My favorite magazine, The Saturday Evening Ghost!
Zombo: Who's your favorite author?
Casper: I don't have one. I prefer ghost writers.

Zombo: What do little ghouls play at parties?
Igor: They play Ghost Office.

Zombo: Where do ghosts go on vacation?
Dr. Shock: Death Valley. They say it's the perfect place for ghouly weds.

Zombo: What's the first thing ghosts should do when they get into a car.
Igor: Fasten their sheet belts?

Zombo: Igor, did you just kick the bucket?
Igor: No, master, but I did turn a little pale.

Old proverb states that you can tell a sick ghost by his coffin.

Zombo: I hear you were the winner of the ghost contest.
Casper: Yeah, I won the Best of Spirits Award.

Zombo: Where does a ghost get his mail?
Zacherley: The dead letter office.

Zombo: What do you call a haunted wigwam?
Zacherley: A creepy teepee.

Zombo: I met a ghost who was seventy-five yesterday.
Dr. Shock: That means next year he'll be a Spirit of '76!

Zombo: How do ghosts notify their friends when they change their address?
Casper: They send out ghost cards.
Zombo: How do you send them?
Casper: By Scare mail.

Zombo: Who tells the scariest ghost stories?
Zacherley: Edgar Allen Boo.

Zombo: Why are Native American ghosts always smiling?
Zacherley: because they've been buried in their happy haunting grounds.

Dr. Shock: So, Casper, who's your favorite doctor?
Casper: Dr. Jekyll.
Dr. Shock: Why him and not me?
Casper: Because he still makes haunted house calls.

Zombo: Have you heard of the ghost that haunts the campus of Transylvania University?
Zacherley: Yes. I refer to him as that old school spirit.

Zombo: What did the ghost do that got picked on at school?
Igor: He went crying to his mummy.

Zombo: Who is the most famous painter in the spirit world?
Zacherley: That would be Vincent van Ghost. He painted the Moaning Lisa.

Zombo: What do ghost writers write on?
Igor: I don't know. What do they write on?
Zombo: They write on tombstones.

Igor: Knock, knock.
Zombo: Who's there?
Igor: Just ghost.
Zombo: Just ghost who?
Igor: Just ghost to show you I can be scary.

First Ghost: I feel a little faint.
Second Ghost: Well, you are white as a sheet.

There once was a ghost named Fred
who didn't mind that he was quite dead.
For something to do
he'd crash a party and shout, "Boo!"
Then he'd watch all of the peoples' faces
turn red.

Tonight's Dinner Menu for the Monsters' Ball

Deviled Eggs
Booloney and Roast Beast Sandwiches
Ghoulash
Smashed Potatoes with Gravey

DRINKS

Evaporated Milk
Whine

DESSERT

Booberry pie with ice scream

CANNIBAL JOKES

Dr. Shock: Did you hear about the cannibal that got expelled from school.
Zombo: Was he putting the bite on his classmates?
Dr. Shock: No. He was buttering up his teacher.
Zombo: Was this the cannibal I say at the All You Can Eat Restaurant yesterday?
Dr. Shock: Yes.
Zombo: What did he have?
Dr. Shock: Two waiters and the busboy.

Zacherley: Did you hear about the cannibal who drank a can of varnish?
Zombo: What happened?
Zacherley: He died, but what a beautiful finish.

Zombo: Waiter! I don't like all these flies in my soup!
Waiter: Well, pick out the ones you do like and I will kill the rest.

Dr. Shock: So how did you become a waiter?
Waiter: Well, I went to butcher school for a while but I couldn't hack it.

First Cannibal: What do you want to do this afternoon?
Second Cannibal: Let's have some friends for lunch.

Zombo: Always stay calm when you meet a cannibal.

Igor: Why?

Zombo: You don't want to get into a stew.

SKELETON JOKES

Zombo: I heard that skeletons don't date much.
Igor: Why is that, master?
Zombo: They have no body to go with.

Igor: I know a skeleton that plays in the band.
Zombo: What instrument does he play?
Igor: The trombone.

Zombo: What kind of games do skeletons like to play?
Igor: I don't know.
Zombo: They like dice games.
Igor: Why?
Zombo: Because they like to roll them bones!

Zombo: Why do skeletons like to listen to early Rock and Roll songs?
Dr. Shock: Because they like to shake, rattle and roll, baby.

Dr. Shock: Who won the skeleton beauty pageant?
Zombo: Nobody.

Zombo: Where do dead sailors usually go?
Igor: I don't know.
Zombo: Why in the Ghost Guard of course!

Zombo: Name a famous monster explorer.
Igor: Daniel Bone for one.

Igor: What do skeletons say to each other before they eat?
Zombo: Bone appetite.

Zombo: What do you call a skeleton who won't work?
Dr. Shock: Lazy bones.

Waitress: Do you want soup or stew?
Skeleton: Soup. Stew sticks to my ribs.

Zombo: And then there was that skeleton that sent away for a body building set.

Igor: Did you hear about the skeleton who got caught in the rainstorm?
Zombo: I'll bet he was soaked to the bone.
Igor: I'll bet a skeleton would laugh at that joke.
Zombo: Why?
Igor: He'd find it a rib tickler.

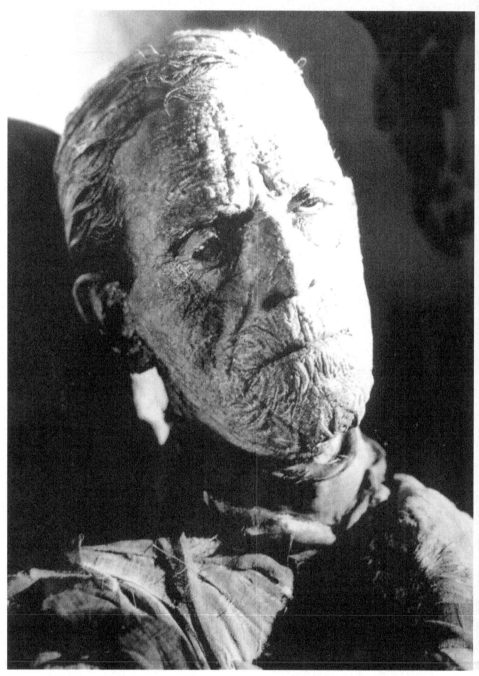

"Why did I have to stay up so late last night?"

MUMMY JOKES

Zombo: What do you call a friendly Egyptian?
Imhotep: A chummy mummy.

Zombo: Is it safe to tell a mummy your darkest secrets?
Imhotep: Of course. He'll keep them under wraps.

Zacherley: How many mummies does it take to change a light bulb?
Zombo: One. But you must watch him because he tends to get wrapped up in his work!

Zombo: What should you do if you don't like a horror movie?
Dr. Shock: Ask for your mummy back.

Zombo: How come the Mummy didn't star in that horror movie?
Zacherley: He couldn't pass the scream test.

Zombo: I heard that King Tut used to like to eat crackers in bed.
Imhotep: Yes. He was a crumby mummy.

I'm worthless without that first cup of coffee.

Kharis: You know that statue that has the head of a man and the body of a lion?
Imhotep: Yes.
Kharis: I noticed that he doesn't have a nose.
Imhotep: How does he smell?
Kharis: Oh, he Sphinx!

Old Proverb states that a ghoul and his mummy are soon parted.

Zombo: Why didn't that mummy join the chorus?
Igor: Because he can't sing. He can't even carry a tomb.

Two mummy's are shuffling along the street when the first mummy asks, "So what did you think of Grant's tomb?"
"Oh," said the second mummy. "It's a nice place but I would-n't want to live there."

Zombo: Dracula added a couple of mummies to his group, The Crypt Kicker Five, for back up vocals.
Zacherley: Pretty smart getting some band aids.

Zombo: Why are there no mummies in the cotton fields down south?
Igor: Because those nasty boll weevils steal and horde them.
Zombo: Oh, I forgot that mummy is the loot of all weevils.

Zombo: From rags to riches is the great American success story.
Imhotep: From riches to rags is the great mummy story.

Zombo: What kind of music do mummies like?
Zacherley: Rag Time.

Imhotep: What is the oldest pyramid?
Kharis: The great Pyramid at Geezer.

Mummies love to have their nails done.

Kharis and Imhotep Present The Secrets of the Pyramids

1. They snore.
2. They never return phone calls.
3. They never tip.
4. They don't like to travel.
5. They watch too much television.
6. They never eat dessert.
7. They won't pay library fines for overdue books.
8. They don't like broccoli.

"Here's a little something for the road."

What is a Horror Host?

A horror host is an entertainer whose job it is to introduce a horror show, play, movie or television program. The host is like an emcee who will tell you the name of the production and probably the actors involved. Most hosts like to handle this job in costume and make up playing the part usually of a frightening creature who, as it turns out, is usually not that frightening. Often jokes and magic tricks are included as part of the Horror Host's routine.

Horror Hosts existed long before television. Many started on the stage presenting what was called a Spook Show. The audience is entertained by the host and whatever ghouls and goblins he brought with him before the main feature, a scary movie is presented. The horror host appeared on radio as well such as one series about an old hermit who lived in a cave and presented scary little radio plays. Horror Hosts even existed in comic books to introduce horror story anthologies.

In the 1950s Vampira rose to fame as the first television Horror Host or Hostess. She introduced viewers in the Los Angeles area to low budget thrillers wrapped around her antics. People watched the program more to see what she was up to rather than what the movie was about.

In 1957 universal Studios released its original horror movies to television under what has become known as the Shock Theatre package. In this package (actually a programming guide book), television stations were encouraged to hire someone to act as a host to introduce these movies and let audiences know that they weren't really that terrifying by making fun of the films. Many stations took this advice and the television Horror Host was born.

Among some of the first Horror Hosts were creatures known as Roland, Tarantula Ghoul, Milton, and Ghoulardi. There were dozens of them in the 1950s. The trend continued in the 1960s and 1970s as well almost dying out until Elvira rose on the West Coast and Stella rose on the East Coast. USA network and later TNT brought hosts back as well. But the most famous Horror Host was the Crypt Keeper from HBO's Tales From the Crypt based upon the 1950s comic book series.

It is in honor of these wonderful people that this Horror Host series of books was created. A series that this author hopes will always remain unfinished see no end as more Horror Hosts continue the tradition of spooky entertainment.

(Special thanks were made by me, Zombo, at the start of this book for the help of two special Horror Hosts who participated in this publication. Their pictures follow. The first is Zacherley, also known as Roland to his friends in Philadelphia, and the second is the frightful Dr. Shock of Philadelphia!)

"Zombo had a hand in bringing me here.!"

"These jokes were worse than the ones on my show."

I, Zombo, recommend the following books for your reading pleasure! You may find them in the finest of places and in the darkest recesses of the monster world. Search for them on Amazon or at a monster show near you.

Collect the entire Horror Host series and more!!!

ZACHERLEY FOR PRESIDENT (AGAIN)

JOHN SKERCHOCK

ZACHERLEY'S
Midnight Monster Tales

by John Skerchock

ZACHERLEY'S
Creature Features

by John Skerchock

Thank you for hanging around with your friend, Zombo. I hope I made you laugh. I hope a chill or two ran up and down your spine. If Zombo failed to entertain you within these pages then it because you are already dead! Ha! Ha! For I am . . .

Zombo!!

-THE END-
Now, please go away!

Made in the USA
Monee, IL
14 April 2022

94749496R20066